First Order of Business

12-Minute Bible Reflections to Open Church Meetings

Judith Marsh Carlson

CHURCH
PUBLISHING
INCORPORATED

Church Publishing
19 East 34th Street
New York, NY 10016

www.churchpublishing.org

Cover design by Jennifer Kopec, 2Pug Design
Typeset by Denise Hoff

Library of Congress Cataloging-in-Publication Data

Names: Carlson, Judith Marsh, author.
Title: First order of business : 12-minute bible reflections to open church
    meetings / Judith Marsh Carlson.
Description: New York, NY : Church Publishing, [2018] | Includes
    bibliographical references and index.
Identifiers: LCCN 2018017821 (print) | LCCN 2018030090 (ebook) |
    ISBN 9781640651067 (ebook) | ISBN 9781640651050 (paperback)
Subjects: LCSH: Church meetings--Prayers and devotions. |
    Bible--Meditations.
Classification: LCC BV652.15 (ebook) | LCC BV652.15 .C37 2018 (print) |
    DDC 264/.7--dc23
LC record available at https://lccn.loc.gov/2018017821

Printed in the United States of America

Contents

Getting Started

BIBLE TRANSLATIONS IN THIS RESOURCE

Three Scripture translations are used in this resource:

New Revised Standard Version (NRSV) Scripture quotations marked "NRSV" are from New Revised Standard Version Bible, copyright © 1989 National Council of the Churches of Christ in the United States of America. Used by permission. All rights reserved worldwide.

The Message Scripture quotations marked "*The Message*" are taken from THE MESSAGE, copyright © 1993, 1994, 1995, 1996, 2000, 2001, 2002 by Eugene H. Peterson. Used by permission of NavPress. All rights reserved. Represented by Tyndale House Publishers, Inc.

Good News Translation (GNB) Scriptures and additional materials quoted and marked "GNB" are from the Good News Bible © 1994 published by the Bible Societies/HarperCollins Publishers Ltd UK, Good News Bible© American Bible Society 1966, 1971, 1976, 1999. Used with permission.

HOW *FIRST ORDER OF BUSINESS* CAME TO BE

Over the years in my work with Episcopal Church groups and ecumenical organizations across the country, I've been consistently impressed by conscientious volunteers and professional staff who go about their many business meetings with determination, even dedication. But I've also been struck over and over by how few of these obviously faithful Christians include even a few minutes of Bible study or other "spiritual component" as a regular part of these meetings—usually a quick opening or closing prayer. Because "it'll take too much time," or they aren't sure what texts to use, or they fear they "don't know enough about the Bible," or somehow they don't feel . . . well, *adequate* for that sort of thing.

Typically these busy people serve generously, often in addition to demanding jobs, family commitments, and other obligations. Clergy too, despite good intentions, have trouble finding *time* to think up, prepare, and perhaps run off something ahead of each meeting. In our over-scheduled era I've heard many speak wistfully of meetings that are "more than just business," then assert ruefully that adding extra agenda would simply mean "too much time." I myself have served on vestries in three different churches—I get it.

TWO CONSTANT CHALLENGES

1. **Is there a simple but authentic method to allow leaders gathered for the church's business to yield a few moments of agenda time to listen to Holy Scriptures and discern what God might be saying to them?**

Simple, because vestry or other committee meetings need no additional complications, no matter how high the purpose.

Authentic, because the baptismal prayer for "an inquiring and discerning heart" means we value times of thoughtful learning, reflection, and sharing to deepen our understanding of God.

2. **Despite obvious benefits, would instituting such a practice regularly at meetings demand more agenda time than is practical or reasonable?**

Participants' time must be respected. Activities must be brief but not superficial, and bring needed contemplative balance to church business meetings.

And so I was determined to see whether a short period—twelve minutes—could be dedicated at the beginning of each gathering to allow some time for the Spirit even in the midst of a dependably demanding agenda.

First Order of Business attempts to address these realities. Here are thirty-six Scripture passages, each with three reflection questions. Leadership (without the need for advance preparation) can be shared among members and is simply a matter of following the open-ended questions after everyone has listened deeply to the text as it is read aloud. Discussion is designed to fit a variety of situations and does not seek pat "right answers." Instead, it is shared conversation among those who are committed to their group's common goals and tasks. The Scripture passages address issues frequently encountered in group life, making faith connections to present-day agenda and concerns. When the twelve minutes are up, the leader, who also serves as timekeeper, closes with a prayer or leads the group in saying "Amen." It's time to move on to business, yet somehow, things are different.

There are the fresh surprises of being intentionally open to the Spirit, but also the chance to hear God's Word and something of each other's inner lives and thoughts, so often unspoken. It's my hope (and experience) that such times of reflection—brief though they are—can transform ordinary "business as usual" into a much broader, richer, more spiritual context for what is after all the holy work of mission and ministry. It was a variant of the approach most frequently known as the "African Bible Study" that offered a workable resolution. It matched the practical needs, and even better, made surprising connections to a host of Christians all across the world, both past and present. To research its history is to discover the imprint of many cultures, traditions, and a very wide range of human situations.

AFRICAN BIBLE STUDY

WHERE IT CAME FROM

Lectio Divina

African Bible Study is a form of *lectio divina*—Latin for "divine reading"—a Benedictine practice more than a thousand years old. It holds that seeking meaning in the Scriptures is not based upon intellectual reasoning or theological analysis but through a process of praying the Scriptures by opening ourselves to God at deep levels.

Its roots trace back to Origen, the third-century Greek theologian and scholar, but it was Guigio, a twelfth-century Carthusian monk in France, who formalized the process into the four commonly known successive stages: *lectio* (reading) where a particular passage of God's Word is read very slowly and reflectively; *meditatio* (reflection) in which the seeker thinks deeply and quietly about the passage selected and ponders what meaning God might want to be received from it at this time; *oratio* (prayer) a turning from reflective thinking to a simple yielding of the heart in order to hear God speak; and *contemplatio* (rest) in which the seeker now gently lets go of all thoughts, even holy ideas, and simply rests at peace in the Word of God.

Although the steps of *lectio divina* have seen many variations, they have never been understood as a fixed set of rules. Yet this prayerful process has attested to the transformative experience of knowing God through Scripture for more than seventeen centuries.

Latin America

It's known as *African*, but one of the origins of African Bible Study was the Latin America of the late 1960s and the social justice movement there (especially in the Roman Catholic Church) known as *liberation theology*. It emerged in response to the extreme poverty and ruthless injustice throughout that region and sought to proclaim the Christian gospel as liberation from these sufferings, especially among the poorest and most oppressed.

Small groups, known as *base communities* and usually of ten to thirty people each, began to spread across Latin America proclaiming this message of freedom, deliverance, and hope. They would study the Scriptures together as they sought to meet the desperate needs of their parishioners. They were particularly concerned with the political and systemic causes of poverty, and thus one of their fundamental focuses was economic. Base community groups were primarily composed of committed laypersons not formally theologically trained, but who became practiced in examining God's Word *from the perspective of people's daily life*. Among those who witnessed the Base Community movement, it was said that liberation theology was "nourished by the underlined bibles of poor and marginalized peasants and urban dwellers."[1]

Even today, with the inescapable changes of the last fifty years, descendant groups of Base Communities are at work serving the Latin American poor, continuing to provide a place where everyday life and faith intersect and are made personal. The combination of

---

1. Quoted by Dr. Lurdino A. Yuzon, Joint Secretary for Council for Mission and Ecumenical Cooperation, Christ Church, Aotearoa-New Zealand, in *Towards a Contextual Theology*, a presentation to the ecumenical Christian Conference of Asia (CCA) and later published in the *CTC Bulletin* by CCA's program area on Faith, Mission, and Unity (Theological Concerns).

reflection and action and the view of faith as intersecting everyday life is a heritage of liberation theology greatly influencing the African Bible Study method.

Africa

Every ten years the bishops of the world's Anglican Church bodies gather to meet together at what is known as the Lambeth Conference to share and consult on issues of the day and to express the mind of their forty-five-member global church Communion. At the 1988 gathering, however, they made a seemingly simple change to the usual routine—in place of the scholarly lectures that had been customary, they decided to begin each day with Bible study in small groups. Planning group members had included bishops from Africa, and it was they who suggested a Bible study method characteristic in churches on their continent. Rather than academic in nature, this approach was reflective and invited participants to examine biblical texts and then share each other's own experiences and personal faith perspectives. Active and deep respectful listening to the words of Scripture and to one another were key to the process.

The Lambeth bishops found what so many others have also discovered: that this very simple practice became for them a valued sacred time to know God and each other more deeply. Many observed afterwards that their relationships with one another as colleagues had been strengthened during this Conference, so much so that ever since they have continued this same practice, having come to recognize it as integral to their mission. Its regular use has now also become a tradition for a number of major Anglican gatherings, including the Episcopal Church's triennial General Convention.

Introducing the African Bible Study method to a global world audience through the Lambeth Conference gave it an exposure that ensured its becoming widely known. Over the years its popularity and use in many settings have naturally produced a number of variations. But it is the simplicity of its process and its focus on Scripture together with holy listening that have made it appealing to Christians in many places and cultures well beyond Africa. Still, "African Bible Study" continues to be the most frequent name by which people designate the versions of this method.

HOW AND WHY THE CHURCH HAS USED IT

Contextual Theology

Scripture and tradition have always been the time-honored sources for understanding Christian faith, but in recent years the insights of contextual theology have added breadth and new awareness. American author, educator, and Roman Catholic priest Stephen B. Bevans defines this movement in his 1992 volume *Models of Contextual Theology*, now recognized as a foundational document for those concerned with how Christian tradition can understand itself in relation to culture. The contextual approach is, he writes,

> a way of doing theology in which one takes into account the spirit and message of the gospel; the tradition of the church; the culture in which one is theologizing; and social change within that culture, whether brought about by western technological process or the grass-roots struggle for equality, justice and liberation.[2]

2. Stephen B. Bevans, *Models of Contextual Theology* (Ossining, NY: Orbis, 1992), 1.

Non-Western Contexts

Because it intentionally looks beyond the western world for theological understandings and includes insights from modern disciplines like psychology, sociology, economics, and political science, contextual theology has a special appeal for peoples in non-Western or developing countries.[3] It has helped them to hear new and clearer echoes of their own particular and unique experiences and so to understand God's presence in their own situations.

Its long struggle against apartheid has caused South Africa to be home to many contextual theologians, and traces of the perspectives of this movement are readily seen in the African Bible Study model. Likewise, Asia, with the magnitude of poverty and suffering in those countries, has produced a number of contextual theologies as Christians there have sought deeply and prayerfully for meaning and hope in their experiences.

Gospel Based Discipleship

Another descendant of the African Bible model—also non-Western—is *Gospel Based Discipleship,* developed in 2000 for the Episcopal Church's Office of Indigenous Ministries and the Anglican Church of Canada. The Rev. John Robertson, then U.S. Missioner for Native/Indigenous Ministries, and the Rt. Rev. Mark McDonald, now National Indigenous Anglican Bishop for the Anglican Church of Canada, along with others, created a format designed to engage people in an encounter with the Gospel. Like the African approach it is simple and direct, can be used with any Bible text, and does not require an experienced leader. An accompanying

---

3. K. C. Abraham, "Third World Theologies," *CTC Bulletin*, May–December 1992, 7.

informational handout says, "The entire faith community" encounters the Gospel as peers, whether ordained or non-ordained . . . [leading] to a vision of the community gathered around the Scripture."[4] A striking originality of this indigenous variation is its intentional blending of worship with Scripture reflection. Materials include *A Disciple's Prayer Book*, designed for liturgical use and patterned after the *Book of Common Prayer's* Daily Office liturgies for seasons of the church year and various times of day. There are psalms and service formats for a gathering, a blessing, and even a vigil for the time of death. *Gospel Based Discipleship* provides many options which are also concise, flexible, adaptable, and easily portable—all these account for its great appeal and use among both indigenous and non-native people alike.

WHAT CHARACTERIZES AFRICAN BIBLE STUDY?

An Inductive Method

The African approach begins, not with the academic, but the particular, by examining a specific biblical passage and drawing from it larger, broader meanings. An inductive method's three stages are clearly evident in the African method—*observation* (what the text says), *interpretation* (what it means), and *application* (what it means to me for my life). A fundamental assumption is a deep connection between our human lives and what Holy Scripture can reveal to us about God and God's purposes for creation. However, one aspect of the African method differs markedly from other inductive Bible study. Deep and active listening is so highly valued and listening so crucial to its pro-

---

4. Online Publicity for *Gospel Based Discipleship* from All Saints Episcopal Indian Mission, Minneapolis, Minnesota, https://allsaintsindianmission.com/gospel-based-discipleship/

cess that there is great respect for what *each person* perceives the text to be saying. Everyone is encouraged to listen and hear something in the text. Others in the group, however, do not comment upon, debate, or criticize what any individual member says. Perceptions are accepted and honored—agreement is not sought. Group members are free from pressures or assumptions about outcomes.

It's important to add here that, regardless of the obvious merits of African Bible Study, it would be a mistake to confine ourselves exclusively to this approach. Faith is strengthened and made richer when we draw upon the assistance and insights from the world of academia and biblical scholarship. Text criticism, biblical history and languages, recognized commentaries—all provide invaluable explanations and interpretations of biblical text. Certainly study needs to be part of faith formation, but it requires at least some time, more than can practically be part of a pre-meeting agenda.

Four Constant Features

Despite a variety of modifications over the years, four distinct steps are generally characteristic.

1. A passage of Scripture is read aloud slowly. Participants in turn mention a word or phrase which has stood out for them as each was listening, but no other comments are made, either by the group or single speakers as they respond.

2. The passage is read aloud again (once or twice), sometimes in a different translation and if possible by someone of a different gender from the first reader. Again, members listen without further comment or discussion—listening, to God and to each other, is the heart of this approach.

3. As others listen, members now share individually, but importantly without comments, discussion, or "crosstalk." Group members disclose as they wish their individual personal responses to individual words and phrases and to the entire text itself, saying how these relate to their life. Some variations ask members to say what action the Bible passage might be suggesting for them personally or what God seems to be calling them as a group to do.

Throughout the process, no matter which version is used, the African Bible Study assumes, as groups listen and study Holy Scripture, that the Holy Spirit is present to bless and guide and inspire them on their journey together. Always African Bible Study sessions end with prayer, both for one another and as a way of concluding their time together.

Like some other alternatives to the African method, *First Order of Business* provides open-ended questions to spark open discussion while nonetheless honoring the promised time limit for reflection. Because such questions do not suggest or imply fixed conclusions, they allow honest responses based, not on some pre-digested "right answers," but on each member's knowledge, experience, and honest feelings. Discussion may be limited in time, but it is certainly free and candid and often meaningful. When a group feels confident that their time and schedule will be dependably honored, when they trust they will be listened to respectfully as they share insights and concerns, then their inclination to allow time for the Spirit in business meetings is likely to result in a regular practice, one that is rewarding beyond the telling.

LEADING THESE BIBLE REFLECTIONS

The easiest and best way is having group members take turns, sharing the leadership at different meetings according to your schedule. Whoever serves as leader simply follows the three steps that come with each Bible passage and also acts as timekeeper.

Step 1. Everyone has a copy of the selected passage and reflection. As the group listens attentively without making any comments, the passage is read aloud in turn by two different readers, preferably of different genders. Hearing the text repeated as well as read in both male and female voices helps the group pay attention more deeply, sometimes hearing the words in fresh and surprising new ways.

Step 2. Watching the time, the leader poses the three reflection questions associated with the passage. The first question is always, "What word, phrase, or thought in this passage particularly strikes you today?," which members are asked to respond to *without any other comments*. The other two questions? They can be answered in any way participants wish within the twelve-minute time frame.

Step 3. When time is up, close with a prayer or simply say "Amen."

Important: Keep the twelve-minute time frame!

It's a covenant that honors every member's personal time and your group's agenda. Discussion is not lengthy, but you'll be surprised how even such a brief time with Scripture transforms the tone and spirit of your meetings together.

And . . . everyone should remember to . . .

- listen courteously always,
- speak for yourself but no one else,
- no cross-talk,
- keep anything said strictly confidential,
- and refrain from judgment.

(It's respectful and the heart of good manners.)

CHOOSING A PASSAGE FOR YOUR MEETING

You can use these Bible passages in any order.

For example, try . . . ..

- A favorite passage (no matter where in the Bible it's located)—something that appeals to you personally or something you want to know more about.

- Going in "Bible Order"—the selections in this resource are arranged in the order in which they appear in most Bibles. Check your Bible's table of contents to be sure.

- A text dealing with a subject or issue relating to your group's or congregation's life at the moment. See the Topical Index of Bible Passages in the back of this resource.

- A Reading that also appears in the appointed Sunday Lectionary close to the date of your meeting. Find a chart entitled Where are these Scriptures in the Sunday RCL Lectionary? also in the back of this resource.

- Something that connects with the current season of the church year.

- Alternating at different meetings between the Hebrew and Christian Scriptures (Old and New Testaments.)

- Simply selecting something at random.

WHAT IF YOUR GROUP HAS ALREADY "USED" A TEXT?

Even if a Scripture text is repeated, you will find that a group's reflections will be different each time—their reactions, their questions, or what members emphasize. Everyone will be "in a different place" personally, and you'll discover even your own responses vary each time as well.

Take heart from the words of Dr. Verna Dozier, the noted Bible teacher and scholar who often reminded students, "Don't try to do it all. The Bible is inexhaustible." That is absolutely true!

Twelve-Minute Reflections

GENESIS 28:10–17 (NRSV)

Jacob left Beer-sheba and went towards Haran. He came to a certain place and stayed there for the night, because the sun had set. Taking one of the stones of the place, he put it under his head and lay down in that place. And he dreamed that there was a ladder set up on the earth, the top of it reaching to heaven; and the angels of God were ascending and descending on it. And the LORD stood beside him and said, "I am the LORD, the God of Abraham your father and the God of Isaac; the land on which you lie I will give to you and to your offspring; and your offspring shall be like the dust of the earth, and you shall spread abroad to the west and to the east and to the north and to the south; and all the families of the earth shall be blessed in you and in your offspring. Know that I am with you and will keep you wherever you go, and will bring you back to this land; for I will not leave you until I have done what I have promised you."

Then Jacob woke from his sleep and said, "Surely the LORD is in this place—and I did not know it!" And he was afraid, and said, "How awesome is this place! This is none other than the house of God, and this is the gate of heaven."

Reflection

1. Listen as the passage is read aloud. Then listen as it is read again, if possible by someone of a different gender.

2. Respond: (10 minutes)
   - What word, phrase, or thought in this passage particularly strikes you today? *(Just the word/phrase—no other comments.)*
   - Have you or someone you've known ever had an experience or an insight similar to Jacob's?

- Jacob is different at the end of this experience, but he's also afraid. What's the cause of his fear, and what is the good news for him?

Close the reflection with prayer or simply say "Amen."

GENESIS 32:24–30 (NRSV)

Jacob was left alone; and a man wrestled with him until daybreak. When the man saw that he did not prevail against Jacob, he struck him on the hip socket; and Jacob's hip was put out of joint as he wrestled with him. Then he said, "Let me go, for the day is breaking." But Jacob said, "I will not let you go, unless you bless me." So he said to him, "What is your name?" And he said, "Jacob." Then the man said, "You shall no longer be called Jacob, but Israel, for you have striven with God and with humans, and have prevailed." Then Jacob asked him, "Please tell me your name." But he said, "Why is it that you ask my name?" And there he blessed him. So Jacob called the place Peniel, saying, "For I have seen God face to face, and yet my life is preserved."

Reflection

1. Listen as the passage is read aloud. Then listen as it is read again, if possible by someone of a different gender.

2. Respond: (10 minutes)

   - What word, phrase, or thought in this passage particularly strikes you today? *(Just the word/phrase—no other comments.)*

   - As a leader (or leaders), can you identify an experience of wrestling with God and others?

- What brings about such wrestling, and how does it leave its mark or change those who go through it?

Close the reflection with prayer or simply say "Amen."

EXODUS 3:7–15 (NRSV)

Then the LORD said [to Moses], "I have observed the misery of my people who are in Egypt; I have heard their cry on account of their taskmasters. Indeed, I know their sufferings, and I have come down to deliver them from the Egyptians, and to bring them up out of that land to a good and broad land, a land flowing with milk and honey, to the country of the Canaanites, the Hittites, the Amorites, the Perizzites, the Hivites, and the Jebusites. The cry of the Israelites has now come to me; I have also seen how the Egyptians oppress them. So come, I will send you to Pharaoh to bring my people, the Israelites, out of Egypt."

But Moses said to God, "Who am I that I should go to Pharaoh, and bring the Israelites out of Egypt?" He said, "I will be with you; and this shall be the sign for you that it is I who sent you: when you have brought the people out of Egypt, you shall worship God on this mountain." But Moses said to God, "If I come to the Israelites and say to them, 'The God of your ancestors has sent me to you,' and they ask me, 'What is his name?' what shall I say to them?" God said to Moses, "I AM WHO I AM." He said further, "Thus you shall say to the Israelites, 'I AM has sent me to you.'" God also said to Moses, "Thus you shall say to the Israelites, 'The LORD, the God of your ancestors, the God of Abraham, the God of Isaac, and the God of Jacob, has sent me to you': This is my name forever, and this my title for all generations."

Reflection

1. Listen as the passage is read aloud. Then listen as it is read again, if possible by someone of a different gender.

2. Respond: (10 minutes)

   • What word, phrase, or thought in this passage particularly strikes you today? *(Just the word/phrase—no other comments.)*

   • What is your reaction to Moses's response to his unexpected assignment?

   • Moses needed a "backup" from God – did he get it?

Close the reflection with prayer or simply say "Amen."

EXODUS 13:17–19 (NRSV)

When Pharaoh let the people go, God did not lead them by way of the land of the Philistines, although that was nearer; for God thought, "If the people face war, they may change their minds and return to Egypt." So God led the people by the roundabout way of the wilderness toward the Red Sea. The Israelites went up out of the land of Egypt prepared for battle. And Moses took with him the bones of Joseph who had required a solemn oath of the Israelites, saying, "God will surely take notice of you, and then you must carry my bones with you from here."

Reflection

1. Listen as the passage is read aloud. Then listen as it is read again, if possible by someone of a different gender.

2. Respond: (10 minutes)

- What word, phrase, or thought in this passage particularly strikes you today? *(Just the word/phrase—no other comments.)*
- Having to go "by the roundabout way"—is this good news? Bad news?
- What would make the people of Israel (or anywhere) decide to carry something like the bones of Joseph with them?

Close the reflection with prayer or simply say "Amen."

EXODUS 18:13–26 (NRSV)

The next day Moses sat as judge for the people, while the people stood around him from morning until evening. When Moses' father-in-law saw all that he was doing for the people, he said, "What is this that you are doing for the people? Why do you sit alone, while all the people stand around you from morning until evening?" Moses said to his father-in-law, "Because the people come to me to inquire of God. When they have a dispute, they come to me and I decide between one person and another, and I make known to them the statutes and instructions of God." Moses' father-in-law said to him, "What you are doing is not good. You will surely wear yourself out, both you and these people with you. For the task is too heavy for you; you cannot do it alone. Now listen to me. I will give you counsel, and God be with you! You should represent the people before God, and you should bring their cases before God; teach them the statutes and instructions and make known to them the way they are to go and the things they are to do. You should also look for able men among all the people, men who fear God, are trustworthy, and hate dishonest gain; set such men over them as officers over thousands, hundreds, fifties and tens. Let them sit as judges for the people at all times; let them bring every important case to you, but decide every minor case themselves. So it will be easier for you, and they will bear the burden with you. If you do this, and God so commands you, then you will be able to endure, and all these people will go to their home in peace." So Moses listened to his father-in-law and did all that he had said. Moses chose able men from all Israel and appointed them as heads over the people, as officers over thousands, hundreds, fifties, and tens. And they judged the people at all times; hard cases they brought to Moses, but any minor case they decided themselves.

Reflection

1. Listen as the passage is read aloud. Then listen as it is read again, if possible by someone of a different gender.

2. Respond: (10 minutes)

   - What word, phrase, or thought in this passage particularly strikes you today? (*Just the word/phrase—no other comments.*)
   - What is challenging about this passage for leaders?
   - What "good news" might this passage have for your church's situation?

Close the reflection with prayer or simply say "Amen."

NUMBERS 11:16-17, 24-29 (NRSV)

So the LORD said to Moses, "Gather for me seventy of the elders of Israel, whom you know to be the elders of the people and officers over them; bring them to the tent of meeting*, and have them take their place there with you. I will come down and talk with you there; and I will take some of the spirit that is on you and put it on them; and they shall bear the burden of the people along with you so that you will not bear it all by yourself."

So Moses went out and told the people the words of the LORD; and he gathered seventy elders of the people, and placed them all around the tent. Then the LORD came down in the cloud and spoke to him, and took some of the spirit that was on him and put it on the seventy elders; and when the spirit rested upon them, they prophesied. But they did not do so again. Two men remained in the camp, one named Eldad, and the other named Medad, and the spirit rested on them; they were among those registered, but they had not gone out to the tent, and so they prophesied in the camp. And a young man ran and told Moses, "Eldad and Medad are prophesying in the camp." And Joshua son of Nun, the assistant of Moses, one of his chosen men, said, "My lord Moses, stop them!" But Moses said to him, "Are you jealous for my sake? Would that all the LORD's people were prophets, and that the LORD would put his spirit on them!"

*The place where Yahweh could be "encountered" or the place where Yahweh's word could be proclaimed to assembled Israel.

Reflection

1. Listen as the passage is read aloud. Then listen as it is read again, if possible by someone of a different gender.

2. Respond: (10 minutes)

   • What word, phrase, or thought in this passage particularly strikes you today? *(Just the word/phrase—no other comments.)*

   • What person in this story did you find yourself interested in or did you identify with?

   • What "leadership issues" within Moses's religious congregation strike you as important here?

Close the reflection with prayer or simply say "Amen."

DEUTERONOMY 6: 1-2, 4-9, 20-25 (NRSV)

Now this is the commandment—the statutes and the ordinances —that the LORD your God charged me to teach you to observe in the land that you are about to cross into and occupy, so that you and your children and your children's children, may fear the LORD your God all the days of your life, and keep all his decrees and his commandments that I am commanding you, so that your days may be long.

Hear, O Israel: The LORD is our God, the LORD alone. You shall love the LORD your God with all your heart, and with all your soul, and with all your might. Keep these words that I am commanding you today in your heart. Recite them to your children and talk about them when you are at home and when you are away, when you lie down and when you rise. Bind them as a sign on your hand, fix them as an emblem on your forehead, and write them on the doorposts of your house and on your gates. When your children ask you in time to come, "What is the meaning of the decrees and the statutes and the ordinances that the LORD our God has commanded you?" then you shall say to your children, "We were Pharaoh's slaves in Egypt, but the LORD brought us out of Egypt with a mighty hand. The LORD displayed before our eyes great and awesome signs and wonders against Egypt, against Pharaoh and all his household. He brought us out from there in order to bring us in, to give us the land that he promised on oath to our ancestors. Then the LORD commanded us to observe all these statutes, to fear the LORD our God, for our lasting good, so as to keep us alive, as is now the case. If we diligently observe this entire commandment before the LORD our God, as he has commanded us, we will be in the right."

Reflection

1. Listen as the passage is read aloud. Then listen as it is read again, if possible by someone of a different gender.

2. Respond: (10 minutes)

   • What word, phrase, or thought in this passage particularly strikes you today? *(Just the word/phrase—no other comments.)*

   • This "recipe for right living" among the people of Israel—is it applicable for people today? Why?

   • "Will you who witness these vows do all in your power to support these persons in their life in Christ?" How does hearing this question at a baptism affect you?

Close the reflection with prayer or simply say "Amen."

1 KINGS 8:1–4, 6, 22–23, 53–58 (NRSV)

The Ark of the Covenant was a wooden chest covered in gold containing the tablets on which the Commandments were inscribed. Built at God's command, it was carried during Israel's desert sojourn, always placed in the Tabernacle where they camped. When Solomon's Temple was built, both the Ark and tablets were permanently placed inside.

Solomon assembled the elders of Israel and all the heads of the tribes . . . to bring up the ark of the covenant of the LORD out of the city of David, which is Zion. All the people of Israel assembled to King Solomon at the festival in the month Ethanim, which is the seventh month. And all the elders of Israel came, and the priests carried the ark. So they brought up the ark of the Lord, the tent of meeting, and all the holy vessels that were in the tent; the priests and the Levites brought them up. Then the priests brought the ark of the covenant of the Lord to its place, in the inner sanctuary of the house, in the most holy place, underneath the wings of the cherubim.

Then Solomon stood before the altar of the LORD in the presence of all the assembly of Israel, and spread out his hands to heaven. He said, "O LORD, God of Israel, there is no God like you in heaven above or on earth beneath, keeping covenant and steadfast love for your servants who walk before you with all their heart. . . . For you have separated them from among all the peoples of the earth, to be your heritage, just as you promised through Moses, your servant, when you brought our ancestors out of Egypt, O LORD God."

Now when Solomon finished offering all this prayer and this

plea to the LORD, he arose from facing the altar of the LORD, where he had knelt with hands outstretched toward heaven; he stood and blessed all the assembly of Israel with a loud voice: "Blessed be the LORD, who has given rest to his people Israel according to all that he promised; not one word has failed of all his good promise, which he spoke through his servant Moses. The LORD our God be with us, as he was with our ancestors; may he not leave us or abandon us, but incline our hearts to him, to walk in all his ways, and to keep his commandments, his statutes, and his ordinances, which he commanded our ancestors."

Reflection

1. Listen as the passage is read aloud. Then listen as it is read again, if possible by someone of a different gender.

2. Respond: (10 minutes)

   • What word, phrase, or thought in this passage particularly strikes you today? *(Just the word/phrase—no other comments.)*

   • Have you ever been part of a grand and historic dedication? What feelings did it evoke among leaders or participants?

   • What have the people of Israel gained? What have they lost?

Close the reflection with prayer or simply say "Amen."

PROVERBS 3:1–7 (NRSV)

My child, do not forget my teaching,
    but let your heart keep my commandments;
for length of days and years of life
    and abundant welfare they will give you.

Do not let loyalty and faithfulness forsake you;
    bind them round your neck,
    write them on the tablet of your heart.
So you will find favor and good repute
    in the sight of God and of people.

Trust in the LORD with all your heart,
    and do not rely on your own insight.
In all your ways acknowledge him,
    and he will make straight your paths.
Do not be wise in your own eyes;
    fear the LORD, and turn away from evil.

Reflection

1. Listen as the passage is read aloud. Then listen as it is read again, if possible by someone of a different gender.

2. Respond: (10 minutes)

   - What word, phrase, or thought in this passage particularly strikes you today? (*Just the word/phrase—no other comments.*)

   - Keeping the Law of Israel often created a doctrine of rewards and punishments, but "loyalty and faithfulness" were also qualities God showed to his people. Which of these is stronger in your congregation's life: doing things "the traditional right way" (laws) or risking something quite new or different to perhaps better fit the situation (faithfulness)?

- Which is more important?
- Based on your own experience, what makes people tend to "rely on their own insight" or be "wise in their own eyes"?

Close the reflection with prayer or simply say "Amen."

ISAIAH 42:5–12, 16 (NRSV)

This first "servant song" talks about the mission of God's servant, chosen to bring forth justice and salvation. It was written at the time when the long exile of the Israelites as slaves in Babylon was ending and their own once mighty city of Jerusalem, now in ruins, was beginning to be restored.

Thus says God, the LORD, who created the heavens and stretched them out, who spread out the earth and what comes from it, who gives breath to the people upon it and spirit to those who walk in it: I am the LORD, I have called you in righteousness, I have taken you by the hand and kept you; I have given you as a covenant to the people, a light to the nations, to open the eyes that are blind, to bring out the prisoners from the dungeon, from the prison those who sit in darkness. I am the LORD, that is my name; my glory I give to no other, nor my praise to idols. See, the former things have come to pass, and new things I now declare; before they spring forth, I tell you of them. Sing to the LORD a new song, his praise from the end of the earth! Let the sea roar and all that fills it, the coastlands and their inhabitants. Let the desert and its towns lift up their voice, the villages that Kedar inhabits; let the inhabitants of Sela sing for joy, let them shout from the tops of the mountains. Let them give glory to the LORD, and declare his praise in the coastlands. I will lead the blind by a road they do not know, by paths they have not known I will guide them. I will turn the darkness before them into light, the rough places into level ground. These are the things I will do, and I will not forsake them.

Reflection

1. Listen as the passage is read aloud. Then listen as it is read again, if possible by someone of a different gender.

2. Respond: (10 minutes)

   • What word, phrase, or thought in this passage particularly strikes you today? *(Just the word/phrase—no other comments.)*

   • As a leader have you ever felt you were walking "blind. . . [on] a road. . . [you] did not know"?

   • When would you say your congregation has needed to hear something like "new things I now declare; before they spring forth, I tell you of them"?

Close the reflection with prayer or simply say "Amen."

JEREMIAH 29:1, 4–14 (NRSV)

These are the words of the letter that the prophet Jeremiah sent from Jerusalem to the remaining elders among the exiles, and to the priests, the prophets, and all the people, whom Nebuchadnezzar had taken into exile from Jerusalem to Babylon

[It said:] Thus says the LORD of hosts, the God of Israel, to all the exiles whom I have sent into exile from Jerusalem to Babylon: Build houses and live in them; plant gardens and eat what they produce. Take wives and have sons and daughters; take wives for your sons, and give your daughters in marriage, that they may bear sons and daughters; multiply there, and do not decrease. But seek the welfare of the city where I have sent you into exile, and pray to the LORD on its behalf, for in its welfare you will find your welfare.

For thus says the LORD of hosts, the God of Israel: Do not let the prophets and the diviners who are among you deceive you, and do not listen to the dreams that they dream, for it is a lie that they are prophesying to you in my name; I did not send them, says the LORD. For thus says the LORD: Only when Babylon's seventy years are completed will I visit you, and I will fulfill to you my promise and bring you back to this place. For surely I know the plans I have for you, says the LORD, plans for your welfare and not for harm, to give you a future with hope. Then when you call upon me and come and pray to me, I will hear you. When you search for me, you will find me; if you seek me with all your heart, I will let you find me, says the LORD, and I will restore your fortunes and gather you from all the nations and all the places where I have driven you, says the LORD, and I will bring you back to the place from which I sent you into exile.

Reflection

1. Listen as the passage is read aloud. Then listen as it is read again, if possible by someone of a different gender.

2. Respond: (10 minutes)

   • What word, phrase, or thought in this passage particularly strikes you today? *(Just the word/phrase—no other comments.)*

   • By definition, exiles aren't where they want to be, either literally or figuratively. If you had heard Jeremiah's advice, how would it have struck you or others in that situation?

   • "Babylon's seventy years," "the place from which I sent you into exile," and "I will restore your fortunes"—what does this tangle of good and bad news mean for them or for you?

Close the reflection with prayer or simply say "Amen."

AMOS 5: 14–15, 21–24 (NRSV)

Seek good and not evil,
that you may live;
and so the LORD, the God of hosts, will be with you,
just as you have said.
Hate evil and love good,
and establish justice in the gate;
it may be that the LORD, the God of hosts,
will be gracious to the remnant of Joseph.

I hate, I despise your festivals,
and I take no delight in your solemn assemblies.
Even though you offer me your burnt-offerings
and grain-offerings,
I will not accept them;
and the offerings of well-being of your fatted animals
I will not look upon.
Take away from me the noise of your songs;
I will not listen to the melody of your harps.
But let justice roll down like waters,
and righteousness like an ever-flowing stream.

Reflection

1. Listen as the passage is read aloud. Then listen as it is read again, if possible by someone of a different gender.

2. Respond: (10 minutes)

   - What word, phrase, or thought in this passage particularly strikes you today? *(Just the word/phrase—no other comments.)*

   - What makes festivals or solemn assemblies "hated or despised" by God?

   - What in the prophet Amos's situation here differs or is like our own circumstances today?

Close the reflection with prayer or simply say "Amen."

MICAH 6:6–8 (NRSV)

"With what shall I come before the **LORD**, and bow myself before God on high? Shall I come before him with burnt offerings, with calves a year old? Will the **LORD** be pleased with thousands of rams, with ten thousands of rivers of oil? Shall I give my firstborn for my transgression, the fruit of my body for the sin of my soul?" He has told you, O mortal, what is good; and what does the **LORD** require of you but to do justice, and to love kindness, and to walk humbly with your God?

Reflection

1. Listen as the passage is read aloud. Then listen as it is read again, if possible by someone of a different gender.

2. Respond: (10 minutes)

   • What word, phrase, or thought in this passage particularly strikes you today? (*Just the word/phrase—no other comments.*)

   • What makes someone ask a question like, "With what shall I come before the Lord?"

   • How does our congregation's mission or our work in this group connect now with what the Lord requires?

Close the reflection with prayer or simply say "Amen."

MATTHEW 5:13–16 (NRSV)

[Jesus said,] "You are the salt of the earth; but if salt has lost its taste, how can its saltiness be restored? It is no longer good for anything, but is thrown out and trampled under foot. "You are the light of the world. A city built on a hill cannot be hid. No one after lighting a lamp puts it under the bushel basket, but on the lampstand, and it gives light to all in the house.

In the same way, let your light shine before others, so that they may see your good works and give glory to your Father in heaven."

Reflection

1. Listen as the passage is read aloud. Then listen as it is read again, if possible by someone of a different gender.

2. Respond: (10 minutes)

   • What word, phrase, or thought in this passage particularly strikes you today? *(Just the word/phrase—no other comments.)*

   • What is salty about this congregation? What could give us more seasoning?

   • Where is the light—what physicists call "luminous energy"—in this congregation? What could make us "shine forth" more brightly?

Close the reflection with prayer or simply say "Amen."

MATTHEW 6:25–34 (NRSV)

[Jesus said,] "Therefore I tell you, do not worry about your life, what you will eat or what you will drink, or about your body, what you will wear. Is not life more than food, and the body more than clothing? Look at the birds of the air; they neither sow nor reap nor gather into barns, and yet your heavenly Father feeds them. Are you not of more value than they? And can any of you by worrying add a single hour to your span of life? And why do you worry about clothing? Consider the lilies of the field, how they grow; they neither toil nor spin, yet I tell you, even Solomon in all his glory was not clothed like one of these. But if God so clothes the grass of the field, which is alive today and tomorrow is thrown into the oven, will he not much more clothe you—you of little faith? Therefore do not worry, saying, 'What will we eat?' or 'What will we drink?' or 'What will we wear?' For it is the Gentiles[5] who strive for all these things; and indeed your heavenly Father knows that you need all these things. But strive first for the kingdom of God and his righteousness, and all these things will be given to you as well. So do not worry about tomorrow, for tomorrow will bring worries of its own. Today's trouble is enough for today."

Reflection

1. Listen as the passage is read aloud. Then listen as it is read again, if possible by someone of a different gender.

2. Respond: (10 minutes)
   - What word, phrase, or thought in this passage particularly strikes you today? (*Just the word/phrase—no other comments.*)
   - Do you find this passage to be unrealistic? Helpful? Impossible? Comforting? Idealistic? Good news?
   - How does it connect to the "worries" of our congregation or our meetings?

Close the reflection with prayer or simply say "Amen."

---

5. Instead of "Gentiles" in verse 32, The Message says, "People who don't know God and the way he works fuss over these things, but you know both God and how he works."

MATTHEW 9:35–38 (NRSV)

Then Jesus went about all the cities and villages, teaching in their synagogues, and proclaiming the good news of the kingdom, and curing every disease and every sickness. When he saw the crowds, he had compassion for them, because they were harassed and helpless, like sheep without a shepherd. Then he said to his disciples, "The harvest is plentiful, but the laborers are few; therefore ask the Lord of the harvest to send out laborers into his harvest."

Reflection

1. Listen as the passage is read aloud. Then listen as it is read again, if possible by someone of a different gender.

2. Respond: (10 minutes)

   • What word, phrase, or thought in this passage particularly strikes you today? *(Just the word/phrase—no other comments.)*

   • What in your community (or the world situation) has aroused feelings of compassion in you recently?

   • "Harassed and helpless," "Sheep without a shepherd," "Send out laborers"—where do these phrases connect, if they do, for you as a church leader today?

Close the reflection with prayer or simply say "Amen."

MATTHEW 11:25–30 (NRSV)

At that time Jesus said, "I thank you, Father, Lord of heaven and earth, because you have hidden these things from the wise and the intelligent and have revealed them to infants; yes, Father, for such was your gracious will. All things have been handed over to me by my Father; and no one knows the Son except the Father, and no one knows the Father except the Son and anyone to whom the Son chooses to reveal him.

"Come to me, all you that are weary and are carrying heavy burdens, and I will give you rest. Take my yoke upon you, and learn from me; for I am gentle and humble in heart, and you will find rest for your souls. For my yoke is easy, and my burden is light."

Reflection

1. Listen as the passage is read aloud. Then listen as it is read again, if possible by someone of a different gender.

2. Respond: (10 minutes)

   - What word, phrase, or thought in this passage particularly strikes you today? *(Just the word/phrase—no other comments.)*

   - Would you say the "Good News" at the end of this passage reflects your experience as busy church leaders "fairly often" or seems "somewhat-true-but-very-idealistic?" How so?

   - How does life in your particular church help or hinder this promise?

Close the reflection with prayer or simply say "Amen."

MATTHEW 18:15-22 (THE MESSAGE)

[Jesus said to his disciples,] "If a fellow believer hurts you, go and tell him—work it out between the two of you. If he listens, you've made a friend. If he won't listen, take one or two others along so that the presence of witnesses will keep things honest, and try again. If he still won't listen, tell the church. If he won't listen to the church, you'll have to start over from scratch, confront him with the need for repentance, and offer again God's forgiving love.

"Take this most seriously: A yes on earth is yes in heaven; a no on earth is no in heaven. What you say to one another is eternal. I mean this. When two of you get together on anything at all on earth and make a prayer of it, my Father in heaven goes into action. And when two or three of you are together because of me, you can be sure that I'll be there."

Reflection

1. Listen as the passage is read aloud. Then listen as it is read again, if possible by someone of a different gender.

2. Respond: (10 minutes)

   • What word, phrase, or thought in this passage particularly strikes you today? *(Just the word/phrase—no other comments.)*

   • Disagreements and hurts have found a way into Christian communities since Jesus's time. How is the approach in this passage reflected (or not) in your congregation's life?

   • What in your experience encourages or discourages such an approach?

Close the reflection with prayer or simply say "Amen."

MATTHEW 20: 20-28 (NRSV)

Then the mother of the sons of Zebedee came to him with her sons, and kneeling before Jesus, she asked a favor of him. And he said to her, "What do you want?" She said to him, "Declare that these two sons of mine will sit, one at your right hand and one at your left, in your kingdom." But Jesus answered, "You do not know what you are asking. Are you able to drink the cup that I am about to drink?" They said to him, "We are able." He said to them, "You will indeed drink my cup, but to sit at my right hand and at my left, this is not mine to grant, but it is for those for whom it has been prepared by my Father."

24 When the ten heard it, they were angry with the two brothers. But Jesus called them to him and said, "You know that the rulers of the Gentiles lord it over them, and their great ones are tyrants over them. It will not be so among you; but whoever wishes to be great among you must be your servant, and whoever wishes to be first among you must be your slave; just as the Son of Man came not to be served but to serve, and to give his life a ransom for many."

Reflection

1. Listen as the passage is read aloud. Then listen as it is read again, if possible by someone of a different gender.

2. Respond: (10 minutes)

   • What word, phrase, or thought in this passage particularly strikes you today? (*Just the word/phrase—no other comments.*)

   • Who do you think is the most interesting character in this story and why?

- What makes a leader valuable? What gives a leader authority?

Close the reflection with prayer or simply say "Amen."

MARK 10:17–27 (NRSV)

As [Jesus] was setting out on a journey, a man ran up and knelt before him, and asked him, "Good Teacher, what must I do to inherit eternal life?" Jesus said to him, "Why do you call me good? No one is good but God alone. You know the commandments: 'You shall not murder; You shall not commit adultery; You shall not steal; You shall not bear false witness; You shall not defraud; Honor your father and mother.'" He said to him, "Teacher, I have kept all these since my youth." Jesus, looking at him, loved him and said, "You lack one thing; go, sell what you own, and give the money to the poor, and you will have treasure in heaven; then come, follow me." When he heard this, he was shocked and went away grieving, for he had many possessions.

Then Jesus looked around and said to his disciples, "How hard it will be for those who have wealth to enter the kingdom of God!" And the disciples were perplexed at these words. But Jesus said to them again, "Children, how hard it is to enter the kingdom of God! It is easier for a camel to go through the eye of a needle than for someone who is rich to enter the kingdom of God." They were greatly astounded and said to one another, "Then who can be saved?" Jesus looked at them and said, "For mortals it is impossible, but not for God; for God all things are possible."

Reflection

1. Listen as the passage is read aloud. Then listen as it is read again, if possible by someone of a different gender.

2. Respond: (10 minutes)

   • What word, phrase, or thought in this passage particularly strikes you today? *(Just the word/phrase—no other comments.)*

   • Is this appealing, rich young man like or unlike most people?

   • What questions or thoughts do you think are going through people's minds in your congregation when they hear this story?

Close the reflection with prayer or simply say "Amen."

LUKE 7:1–10 (NRSV)

Note: A centurion was the captain of a company of a hundred men in the Roman legion (and a gentile).

After Jesus had finished all his sayings in the hearing of the people, he entered Capernaum. A centurion there had a slave whom he valued highly, and who was ill and close to death. When he heard about Jesus, he sent some Jewish elders to him, asking him to come and heal his slave. When they came to Jesus, they appealed to him earnestly, saying, "He is worthy of having you do this for him, for he loves our people, and it is he who built our synagogue for us." And Jesus went with them, but when he was not far from the house, the centurion sent friends to say to him, "Lord, do not trouble yourself, for I am not worthy to have you come under my roof; therefore I did not presume to come to you. But only speak the word, and let my servant be healed. For I also am a man set under authority, with soldiers under me; and I say to one, 'Go,' and he goes, and to another, 'Come,' and he comes, and to my slave, 'Do this,' and the slave does it." When Jesus heard this he was amazed at him, and turning to the crowd that followed him, he said, "I tell you, not even in Israel have I found such faith." When those who had been sent returned to the house, they found the slave in good health.

Reflection

1. Listen as the passage is read aloud. Then listen as it is read again, if possible by someone of a different gender.

2. Respond: (10 minutes)

   • What word, phrase, or thought in this passage particularly strikes you today? *(Just the word/phrase— no other comments.)*

   • Others had faith, so what was so amazing to Jesus about this centurion?

   • Have you known someone with this sort of faith?

Close the reflection with prayer or simply say "Amen."

LUKE 16:1–13 (THE MESSAGE)

Jesus said to his disciples, "There was once a rich man who had a manager. He got reports that the manager had been taking advantage of his position by running up huge personal expenses. So he called him in and said, 'What's this I hear about you? You're fired. And I want a complete audit of your books.'

"The manager said to himself, 'What am I going to do? I've lost my job as manager. I'm not strong enough for a laboring job, and I'm too proud to beg. . . . Ah, I've got a plan. Here's what I'll do . . . then when I'm turned out into the street, people will take me into their houses.'

"Then he went at it. One after another, he called in the people who were in debt to his master. He said to the first, 'How much do you owe my master?'

"He replied, 'A hundred jugs of olive oil.'

"The manager said, 'Here, take your bill, sit down here—quick now— write fifty.'

"To the next he said, 'And you, what do you owe?'

"He answered, 'A hundred sacks of wheat.'

"He said, 'Take your bill, write in eighty.'

"Now here's a surprise: The master praised the crooked manager! And why? Because he knew how to look after himself. Streetwise people are smarter in this regard than law-abiding citizens. They are on constant alert, looking for angles, surviving by their wits. I want you to be smart in the same way—but for what is *right*—using every adversity to stimulate you to creative survival, to concentrate your attention on the bare essentials, so you'll live, really live, and not complacently just get by on good behavior."

Jesus went on to make these comments:

> If you're honest in small things,
> you'll be honest in big things;
> If you're a crook in small things,
> you'll be a crook in big things.
> If you're not honest in small jobs,
> who will put you in charge of the store?
> No worker can serve two bosses:
> He'll either hate the first and love the second
> Or adore the first and despise the second.
> You can't serve both God and the Bank.

Reflection

1. Listen as the passage is read aloud. Then listen as it is read again, if possible by someone of a different gender.

2. Respond: (10 minutes)
   - What word, phrase, or thought in this passage particularly strikes you today? *(Just the word/phrase—no other comments.)*
   - How do you react to Jesus's comment that "Streetwise people are smarter in this regard than law-abiding citizens." What is being admired here?
   - Have you known people who use "every adversity to stimulate…[themselves] to creative survival, to concentrate…attention on the bare essentials"? What did you think of them?

Close the reflection with prayer or simply say "Amen."

LUKE 19:1–10 (NRSV)

Jesus entered Jericho and was passing through it. A man was there named Zacchaeus; he was a chief tax collector and was rich. He was trying to see who Jesus was, but on account of the crowd he could not, because he was short in stature. So he ran ahead and climbed a sycamore tree to see him, because he was going to pass that way. When Jesus came to the place, he looked up and said to him, "Zacchaeus, hurry and come down; for I must stay at your house today." So he hurried down and was happy to welcome him. All who saw it began to grumble and said, "He has gone to be the guest of one who is a sinner." Zacchaeus stood there and said to the Lord, "Look, half of my possessions, Lord, I will give to the poor; and if I have defrauded anyone of anything, I will pay back four times as much." Then Jesus said to him, "Today salvation has come to this house, because he too is a son of Abraham. For the Son of Man came to seek out and to save the lost."

Tax collectors bid for territories in which they could collect local taxes for the Romans, then highly inflate the actual rates, and keep large profits for themselves.

Reflection

1. Listen as the passage is read aloud. Then listen as it is read again, if possible by someone of a different gender.

2. Respond: (10 minutes)

   • What word, phrase, or thought in this passage particularly strikes you today? *(Just the word/phrase—no other comments.)*

- If you had been there, would you have been a grumbler? Do you feel that in this case grumbling was appropriate? Out of line? Too judgmental? Something else?
- How do you explain the change in Zacchaeus? Have you ever known of anyone who underwent a similar transformation?

Close the reflection with prayer or simply say "Amen."

JOHN 15:1–11 (NRSV)

[Jesus declared to his disciples,] "I am the true vine, and my Father is the vine-grower. He removes every branch in me that bears no fruit. Every branch that bears fruit he prunes to make it bear more fruit. You have already been cleansed by the word that I have spoken to you. Abide in me as I abide in you. Just as the branch cannot bear fruit by itself unless it abides in the vine, neither can you unless you abide in me. I am the vine, you are the branches. Those who abide in me and I in them bear much fruit, because apart from me you can do nothing. Whoever does not abide in me is thrown away like a branch and withers; such branches are gathered, thrown into the fire, and burned. If you abide in me, and my words abide in you, ask for whatever you wish, and it will be done for you. My Father is glorified by this, that you bear much fruit and become my disciples.

As the Father has loved me, so I have loved you; abide in my love. If you keep my commandments, you will abide in my love, just as I have kept my Father's commandments and abide in his love. I have said these things to you so that my joy may be in you, and that your joy may be complete."

Reflection

1. Listen as the passage is read aloud. Then listen as it is read again, if possible by someone of a different gender.

2. Respond: (10 minutes)

   • What word, phrase, or thought in this passage particularly strikes you today? *(Just the word/phrase—no other comments.)*

   • Does anything in this passage speaks to you personally as a leader?

   • What "good news" might this passage offer to you and your parishioners at this point in your church's life? What challenges?

Close the reflection with prayer or simply say "Amen."

JOHN 15:12–17 (NRSV)

[Jesus said,] "This is my commandment, that you love one another as I have loved you. No one has greater love than this, to lay down one's life for one's friends. You are my friends if you do what I command you. I do not call you servants any longer, because the servant does not know what the master is doing; but I have called you friends, because I have made known to you everything that I have heard from my Father. You did not choose me but I chose you. And I appointed you to go and bear fruit, fruit that will last, so that the Father will give you whatever you ask him in my name. I am giving you these commands so that you may love one another."

Reflection

1. Listen as the passage is read aloud. Then listen as it is read again, if possible by someone of a different gender.

2. Respond: (10 minutes)

   - What word, phrase, or thought in this passage particularly strikes you today? *(Just the word/phrase—no other comments.)*

   - What could this passage suggest to you about church leaders? About the purpose of this meeting or of this group?

   - What does being *chosen* or called a *friend* imply to you? Does it feel "real"?

Close the reflection with prayer or simply say "Amen."

JOHN 16:12–15 (GNB)

"I have much more to tell you, but now it would be too much for you to bear. When, however, the Spirit comes, who reveals the truth about God, he will lead you into all the truth. He will not speak on his own authority, but he will speak of what he hears and will tell you of things to come. He will give me glory, because he will take what I say and tell it to you. All that my Father has is mine; that is why I said that the Spirit will take what I give him and tell it to you."

Reflection

1. Listen as the passage is read aloud. Then listen as it is read again, if possible by someone of a different gender.

2. Respond: (10 minutes)

- What word, phrase, or thought in this passage particularly strikes you today? *(Just the word/phrase—no other comments.)*
- Do you suppose most people in your church would be confused or encouraged by this passage? Why?
- What in this promise of Jesus could be considered relevant to church leaders or to people in general in today's world?

Close the reflection with prayer or simply say "Amen."

ACTS 3:12B–21 (NRSV)

When Peter saw it, he addressed the people, "[. . .] The God of Abraham, the God of Isaac, and the God of Jacob, the God of our ancestors has glorified his servant Jesus, whom you handed over and rejected in the presence of Pilate. . . and you killed the Author of life, whom God raised from the dead. To this we are witnesses. And now, friends, I know that you acted in ignorance, as did also your rulers. In this way God fulfilled what he had foretold through all the prophets, that his Messiah would suffer. Repent therefore, and turn to God so that your sins may be wiped out, so that times of refreshing may come from the presence of the Lord, and that he may send the Messiah appointed for you, that is, Jesus, who must remain in heaven until the time of universal restoration that God announced long ago through his holy prophets."

Reflection

1. Listen as the passage is read aloud. Then listen as it is read again, if possible by someone of a different gender.

2. Respond: (10 minutes)

- What word, phrase, or thought in this passage particularly strikes you today? *(Just the word/phrase—no other comments.)*

- It is likely that everyone at times experiences a deep longing for "times of refreshing." How does our congregation respond to this longing? What promotes or gets in the way of knowing this refreshment from the Lord's presence?

- Regarding the "time of universal restoration": Do you think most Christians have an active expectation about this or more of an "I sure hope so" attitude? What determines their perspectives?

Close the reflection with prayer or simply say "Amen."

ACTS 11:1–18 (NRSV)

Now the apostles and the believers who were in Judea heard that the Gentiles had also accepted the word of God. So when Peter went up to Jerusalem, the circumcised believers criticized him, saying, "Why did you go to uncircumcised men and eat with them?" Then Peter began to explain it to them, step by step, saying, "I was in the city of Joppa praying, and in a trance I saw a vision. There was something like a large sheet coming down from heaven, being lowered by its four corners; and it came close to me. As I looked at it closely I saw four-footed animals, beasts of prey, reptiles, and birds of the air. I also heard a voice saying to me, 'Get up, Peter; kill and eat.' But I replied, 'By no means, Lord; for nothing profane or unclean has ever entered my mouth.' But a second time the voice answered from heaven, 'What God has made clean, you must not call profane.' This happened three times; then everything was pulled up again to heaven. At that very moment three men, sent to me from Caesarea, arrived at the house where we were. The Spirit told me to go with them and not to make a distinction between them and us. These six brothers also accompanied me, and we entered the man's house. He told us how he had seen the angel standing in his house and saying, 'Send to Joppa and bring Simon, who is called Peter; he will give you a message by which you and your entire household will be saved.' And as I began to speak, the Holy Spirit fell upon them just as it had upon us at the beginning. And I remembered the word of the Lord, how he had said, 'John baptized with water, but you will be baptized with the Holy Spirit.' If then God gave them the same gift that he gave us when we believed in the Lord Jesus Christ, who was I that I could hinder God?" When they heard this, they were silenced. And they praised God, saying, "Then God has given even to the Gentiles the repentance that leads to life."

Reflection

1. Listen as the passage is read aloud. Then listen as it is read again, if possible by someone of a different gender.

2. Respond: (10 minutes)

   • What word, phrase, or thought in this passage particularly strikes you today? (*Just the word/phrase—no other comments.*)

   • What character or group in this story did you find yourself identifying with and why (or not)?

   • What kinds of things would various characters (or people today) have to deal with after they absorb the implication of Peter's explanation?

Close the reflection with prayer or simply say "Amen."

1 CORINTHIANS 1:10–18 (NRSV)

Now I appeal to you, brothers and sisters, by the name of our Lord Jesus Christ, that all of you be in agreement and that there be no divisions among you, but that you be united in the same mind and the same purpose. For it has been reported to me by Chloe's people that there are quarrels among you, my brothers and sisters. What I mean is that each of you says, "I belong to Paul," or "I belong to Apollos," or "I belong to Cephas," or "I belong to Christ." Has Christ been divided? Was Paul crucified for you? Or were you baptized in the name of Paul?

I thank God that I baptized none of you except Crispus and Gaius, so that no one can say that you were baptized in my name. (I did baptize also the household of Stephanas; beyond that, I do not know whether I baptized anyone else.)

For Christ did not send me to baptize but to proclaim the gospel, and not with eloquent wisdom, so that the cross of Christ might not be emptied of its power. For the message about the cross is foolishness to those who are perishing, but to us who are being saved it is the power of God.

Reflection

1. Listen as the passage is read aloud. Then listen as it is read again, if possible by someone of a different gender.

2. Respond: (10 minutes)

   • What word, phrase, or thought in this passage particularly strikes you today? (*Just the word/phrase— no other comments.*)

   • What about these Corinthian congregations compares to your own congregation or others you have known?

- Now, as then, conflicts inevitably arise. Do you believe that people can be truly honest about their varying views and "be in agreement and. . . united in the same mind and the same purpose"? What allows this to happen?

Close the reflection with prayer or simply say "Amen."

1 CORINTHIANS 2:1–10 (THE MESSAGE)

You'll remember, friends, that when I [Paul] first came to you to let you in on God's master stroke, I didn't try to impress you with polished speeches and the latest philosophy. I deliberately kept it plain and simple: first Jesus and who he is; then Jesus and what he did—Jesus crucified.

I was unsure of how to go about this, and felt totally inadequate—I was scared to death, if you want the truth of it—and so nothing I said could have impressed you or anyone else. But the Message came through anyway. God's Spirit and God's power did it, which made it clear that your life of faith is a response to God's power, not to some fancy mental or emotional footwork by me or anyone else.

We, of course, have plenty of wisdom to pass on to you once you get your feet on firm spiritual ground, but it's not popular wisdom, the fashionable wisdom of high-priced experts that will be out-of-date in a year or so. God's wisdom is something mysterious that goes deep into the interior of his purposes. You don't find it lying around on the surface. It's not the latest message, but more like the oldest—what God determined as the way to bring out his best in us, long before we ever arrived on the scene. The experts of our day haven't a clue about what this eternal plan is. If they had, they wouldn't have killed the Master of the God-designed life on a cross. That's why we have this Scripture text: "No one's ever seen or heard anything like this, Never so much as imagined anything quite like it— What God has arranged for those who love him." [cf. Is. 64:4]

But *you've* seen and heard it because God by his Spirit has brought it all out into the open before you. The Spirit, not content to flit around on the surface, dives into the depths of God, and brings out what God planned all along.

Reflection

1. Listen as the passage is read aloud. Then listen as it is read again, if possible by someone of a different gender.

2. Respond: (10 minutes)

   • What word, phrase, or thought in this passage particularly strikes you today? *(Just the word/phrase— no other comments.)*

   • Paul was "unsure," "totally inadequate," "scared to death . . . but the Message came through anyway." Was he just lucky? Unusually talented? Do you believe this only worked for Paul?

   • What about the Christian message would you describe as not "popular" (or fashionable) wisdom or not "lying around on the surface"?

Close the reflection with prayer or simply say "Amen."

1 CORINTHIANS 3:1–11 (NRSV)

And so, brothers and sisters, I could not speak to you as spiritual people, but rather as people of the flesh, as infants in Christ. I fed you with milk, not solid food, for you were not ready for solid food. Even now you are still not ready, for you are still of the flesh. For as long as there is jealousy and quarreling among you, are you not of the flesh, and behaving according to human inclinations? For when one says, "I belong to Paul," and another, "I belong to Apollos," are you not merely human?

What then is Apollos? What is Paul? Servants through whom you came to believe, as the Lord assigned to each. I planted, Apollos watered, but God gave the growth. So neither the one who plants nor the one who waters is anything, but only God who gives the growth. The one who plants and the one who waters have a common purpose, and each will receive wages according to the labor of each. For we are God's servants, working together; you are God's field, God's building. According to the grace of God given to me, like a skilled master builder I laid a foundation, and someone else is building on it. Each builder must choose with care how to build on it. For no one can lay any foundation other than the one that has been laid; that foundation is Jesus Christ.

Reflection

1. Listen as the passage is read aloud. Then listen as it is read again, if possible by someone of a different gender.

2. Respond: (10 minutes)

   • What word, phrase, or thought in this passage particularly strikes you today? *(Just the word/phrase—no other comments.)*

- Is your congregation consuming more "milk" or "solid food"? Why do you say this, and has it mostly been this way or is there a change? Does the group mostly agree?

- Do you think your parishioners with different responsibilities understand clearly that they share a common purpose? What helps or hinders being able to work as "spiritual people" (mature Christians)?

Close the reflection with prayer or simply say "Amen."

1 CORINTHIANS 12:1–11 (THE MESSAGE)

[Paul's letter continues:] What I want to talk about now is the various ways God's Spirit gets worked into our lives. This is complex and often misunderstood, but I want you to be informed and knowledgeable. Remember how you were when you didn't know God, led from one phony god to another, never knowing what you were doing, just doing it because everybody else did it? It's different in this life. God wants us to use our intelligence, to seek to understand as well as we can. For instance, by using your heads, you know perfectly well that the Spirit of God would never prompt anyone to say "Jesus be damned!" Nor would anyone be inclined to say "Jesus is Master!" without the insight of the Holy Spirit.

God's various gifts are handed out everywhere; but they all originate in God's Spirit. God's various ministries are carried out everywhere; but they all originate in God's Spirit. God's various expressions of power are in action everywhere; but God himself is behind it all. Each person is given something to do that shows who God is: Everyone gets in on it, everyone benefits. All kinds of things are handed out by the Spirit, and to all kinds of people! The variety is wonderful:

> wise counsel
> clear understanding
> simple trust
> healing the sick
> miraculous acts
> proclamation
> distinguishing between spirits
> tongues
> interpretation of tongues.

All these gifts have a common origin, but are handed out one by one by the one Spirit of God. He decides who gets what, and when.

Reflection

1. Listen as the passage is read aloud. Then listen as it is read again, if possible by someone of a different gender.

2. Respond: (10 minutes)

   - What word, phrase, or thought in this passage particularly strikes you today? (*Just the word/phrase—no other comments.*)
   - How would you say this picture of people and their gifts is actually lived out in your church's life? How could it be strengthened?
   - What about this passage could be "Good News" for you and your congregation (or for our neighboring community) and what might be a surprise?

Close the reflection with prayer or simply say "Amen."

PHILIPPIANS 4:4–9 (NRSV)

Rejoice in the Lord always; again I will say, Rejoice. Let your gentleness be known to everyone. The Lord is near. Do not worry about anything, but in everything by prayer and supplication with thanksgiving let your requests be made known to God. And the peace of God, which surpasses all understanding, will guard your hearts and your minds in Christ Jesus. Finally, beloved, whatever is true, whatever is honorable, whatever is just, whatever is pure, whatever is pleasing, whatever is commendable, if there is any excellence and if there is anything worthy of praise, think about these things. Keep on doing the things that you have learned and received and heard and seen in me, and the God of peace will be with you.

Reflection

1. Listen as the passage is read aloud. Then listen as it is read again, if possible by someone of a different gender.

2. Respond: (10 minutes)

   - What word, phrase, or thought in this passage particularly strikes you today? *(Just the word/phrase—no other comments.)*

   - "Do not worry about anything. . . . " Is this possible? Realistic? Asking too much?

   - Is someone who thinks about the true, honorable, just, pure, pleasing, and so on wearing "rose-colored glasses"? What about leaders "facing the facts"?

Close the reflection with prayer or simply say "Amen."

COLOSSIANS 3:8–17 (NRSV)

But now you must get rid of all such things—anger, wrath, malice, slander, and abusive language from your mouth. Do not lie to one another, seeing that you have stripped off the old self with its practices and have clothed yourselves with the new self, which is being renewed in knowledge according to the image of its creator. In that renewal there is no longer Greek and Jew, circumcised and uncircumcised, barbarian, Scythian, slave and free; but Christ is all and in all!

As God's chosen ones, holy and beloved, clothe yourselves with compassion, kindness, humility, meekness, and patience. Bear with one another and, if anyone has a complaint against another, forgive each other; just as the Lord has forgiven you, so you also must forgive. Above all, clothe yourselves with love, which binds everything together in perfect harmony. And let the peace of Christ rule in your hearts, to which indeed you were called in the one body. And be thankful. Let the word of Christ dwell in you richly; teach and admonish one another in all wisdom; and with gratitude in your hearts sing psalms, hymns, and spiritual songs to God. And whatever you do, in word or deed, do everything in the name of the Lord Jesus, giving thanks to God the Father through him.

Reflection

1. Listen as the passage is read aloud. Then listen as it is read again, if possible by someone of a different gender.

2. Respond: (10 minutes)

   • What word, phrase, or thought in this passage particularly strikes you today? (*Just the word/phrase—no other comments.*)

- What reaction(s) does this passage evoke in you? Good news or idealism? Unattainable, inspiring, or something else?
- What hopes or hurdles do you see in this passage for you as "real life" church leaders?

Close the reflection with prayer or simply say "Amen."

2 TIMOTHY 1:1–14A (NRSV)

Paul, an apostle of Christ Jesus by the will of God, for the sake of the promise of life that is in Christ Jesus, To Timothy, my beloved child: Grace, mercy, and peace from God the Father and Christ Jesus our Lord. I am grateful to God—whom I worship with a clear conscience, as my ancestors did—when I remember you constantly in my prayers night and day. Recalling your tears, I long to see you so that I may be filled with joy. I am reminded of your sincere faith, a faith that lived first in your grandmother Lois and your mother Eunice and now, I am sure, lives in you.

For this reason I remind you to rekindle the gift of God that is within you through the laying on of my hands; for God did not give us a spirit of cowardice, but rather a spirit of power and of love and of self-discipline. Do not be ashamed, then, of the testimony about our Lord or of me his prisoner, but join with me in suffering for the gospel, relying on the power of God, who saved us and called us with a holy calling, not according to our works but according to his own purpose and grace.

Reflection

1. Listen as the passage is read aloud. Then listen as it is read again, if possible by someone of a different gender.

2. Respond: (10 minutes)

   • What word, phrase, or thought in this passage particularly strikes you today? *(Just the word/phrase— no other comments.)*

   • Whom would you name in your own life or in your congregation as people from whom you've received a "faith that first lived in them?" Are they conscious of their influence or not?

   • Paul says, "Do not be ashamed" and also reminds Timothy "to rekindle the gift of God that is within you . . . for God did not give us a spirit of cowardice, but . . . a spirit of power and of love and of self-discipline." Is this a pep talk to try harder? Nike's "Just do it"? Or something else?

Close the reflection with prayer or simply say "Amen."

JAMES 2:1–13 (NRSV)

My brothers and sisters, do you with your acts of favoritism really believe in our glorious Lord Jesus Christ? For if a person with gold rings and in fine clothes comes into your assembly, and if a poor person in dirty clothes also comes in, and if you take notice of the one wearing the fine clothes and say, "Have a seat here, please", while to the one who is poor you say, "Stand there", or, "Sit at my feet", have you not made distinctions among yourselves, and become judges with evil thoughts? Listen, my beloved brothers and sisters. Has not God chosen the poor in the world to be rich in faith and to be heirs of the kingdom that he has promised to those who love him? But you have dishonored the poor. Is it not the rich who oppress you? Is it not they who drag you into court? Is it not they who blaspheme the excellent name that was invoked over you?

You do well if you really fulfill the royal law according to the scripture, "You shall love your neighbor as yourself." But if you show partiality, you commit sin and are convicted by the law as transgressors. For whoever keeps the whole law but fails in one point has become accountable for all of it. For the one who said, "You shall not commit adultery", also said, "You shall not murder." Now if you do not commit adultery but if you murder, you have become a transgressor of the law. So speak and so act as those who are to be judged by the law of liberty. For judgment will be without mercy to anyone who has shown no mercy; mercy triumphs over judgment.

Reflection

1. Listen as the passage is read aloud. Then listen as it is read again, if possible by someone of a different gender.

2. Respond: (10 minutes)

   • What word, phrase, or thought in this passage particularly strikes you today? (*Just the word/phrase—no other comments.*)

   • Where would you find oppression, partiality, or mercy where you live today?

   • Looking at your congregation, what do you think they might find difficult about welcoming newcomers or people from your community? What kind of "partiality" might seem tempting to them (or you)?

Close the reflection with prayer or simply say "Amen."

Concluding Prayers

Almighty and Eternal God, who sustains and renews this parish family: Empower us through your Spirit as we seek to discover and live out the mission of our congregation. Grant us vision and wisdom to discern your will, patience and resolve to fulfill it faithfully, and energy and trust for the journey, wherever in your love you lead us. All this we ask through Jesus Christ our Lord. *Amen.*

Living God, you meet us in the presence of Jesus the Christ. Prepare us for our meeting together [at . . . .] Bless this holy meeting. Make it a base for mission and ministry. Make it a base for peace and unity. Make it a base for grace and generosity. Make it a base for holiness and hospitality. And give us each the true humility to say, Begin with me. *Amen.*

> *Beginning daily prayer, A Novena for the Lambeth Conference,*
> *1998 Lambeth bishops' prayer booklet, adapted, with permission.*

FROM THE BOOK OF COMMON PRAYER

The grace of our Lord Jesus Christ, and the love of God, and the fellowship of the Holy Spirit, be with us all evermore. *Amen.*

> *2 Corinthians 13:14*
> *Morning Prayer II, p. 102*

May the God of hope fill us with all joy and peace in believing through the power of the Holy Spirit. *Amen.*

Romans 15:13
Morning Prayer II, p.102

Glory to God whose power, working in us, can do infinitely more than we can ask or imagine: Glory to him from generation to generation in the Church, and in Christ Jesus for ever and ever. *Amen.*

Ephesians 3:20,21
Morning Prayer II, p. 102

Lord, you now have set your servant free
>to go in peace as you have promised;

For these eyes of mine have seen the Savior,
whom you have prepared for all the
>world to see:

A Light to enlighten the nations,
>and the glory of your people Israel.

Glory to the Father, and to the Son,
>and to the Holy Spirit:

as it was in the beginning, is now,
>and will be for ever. *Amen.*

Luke 2:29–32, The Song of Simeon (Nunc Dimittis)
Evening Prayer II, p. 120; Compline, p. 13;
Devotions At the Close of Day, p.140.

Almighty God, to whom our needs are known before we ask: help us to ask only what accords with your will; and those good things which we dare not, or in our blindness cannot ask, grant us for the sake of your Son Jesus Christ our Lord. *Amen.*

Collect 4 at the Prayers of the People
p.394

Gracious Father, we pray for thy holy Catholic Church. Fill it with all truth, in all truth with all peace. Where it is corrupt, purify it; where it is in error, direct it; where in any thing it is amiss, reform it. Where it is right, strengthen it; where it is in want, provide for it; where it is divided, reunite it; for the sake of Jesus Christ thy Son our Savior. *Amen.*

Prayers for the Church, 7
p.816

Almighty and everliving God, ruler of all things in heaven and earth, hear our prayers for this parish family. Strengthen the faithful, arouse the careless, and restore the penitent. Grant us all things necessary for our common life, and bring us all to be of one heart and mind within your holy Church; through Jesus Christ our Lord. *Amen.*

Prayers for the Church, 11
p.817

Almighty and everliving God, source of all wisdom and understanding, be present with those who take counsel [in _____] for the renewal and mission of your Church. Teach us in all things to seek first your honor and glory. Guide us to perceive what is right, and grant us both the courage to pursue it and the grace to accomplish it; through Jesus Christ our Lord. *Amen.*

Prayers for the Church, 12
p. 818

Direct us, O Lord, in all our doings with thy most gracious favor, and further us with thy continual help; that in all our works begun, continued, and ended in thee, we may glorify thy holy Name, and finally, by thy mercy, obtain everlasting life; through Jesus Christ our Lord. *Amen.*

Prayers, 57 For Guidance
p. 832

O God, by whom the meek are guided in judgment, and light rises up in darkness for the godly: Grant us, in all our doubts and uncertainties, the grace to ask what you would have us to do, that the Spirit of wisdom may save us from all false choices, and that in your light we may see light, and in your straight path may not stumble; through Jesus Christ our Lord. *Amen.*

Prayers, 58 For Guidance
p. 832

Indices and Aids
to Using This Book

BIBLE PASSAGES FROM THE OLD TESTAMENT

BIBLE PASSAGES FROM THE NEW TESTAMENT

WHERE ARE THESE PASSAGES IN THE SUNDAY REVISED COMMON LECTIONARY*?

The Bible readings in The Revised Common Lectionary (RCL) are used in worship according to the Christian liturgical calendar. Based on the 1969 *Ordo Lectionum Missae*, the RCL began as a three-year lectionary produced by the Roman Catholic Church after Vatican II. Today, some fifty years later, it continues in local translations as the standard Roman Catholic lectionary and in regular use by thirty-seven Protestant denominations around the world, in original or adapted form. Using the RCL every Sunday are denominations in the United States (13), Canada (6), United Kingdom (6), Philippines (6), Australia (2), and Italy (4). You can find the texts in this resource listed in "bible order" next to the days on which they appear in the Sunday RCL.

Passage	Revised Common Lectionary
Genesis 28:10–17	St. Michael and All Angels (September 29)
	Year A—Proper 11
Genesis 32:24–30	Year A—Proper 13
	Year C—Proper 24
Exodus 3:7–12	Year C—Lent 3
	Year A—Proper 17
Exodus 13:17–19	Does not appear
Exodus 18:13–26	Does not appear
Numbers 11:16–17, 24–29	Year B—Proper 21
Deuteronomy 6:1–2, 4–9,20–25	Year B—Proper 26
1 Kings 8:1–6, 9, 22–23, 53–58	Year B—Proper 16
Proverbs 3:1–7	St. Matthew (September 21)
Isaiah 42:5–12,16	St. Barnabas (June 11)
Jeremiah 29:1, 4–14	Year C—Proper 23

Amos 5:14–15, 21–24	Year A—Proper 27
	Year B—Proper 23
Micah 6:6–8	Year a—Epiphany 4
Matthew 5:13–16	Year A—Epiphany 5
Matthew 6:25–34	Year A—Epiphany
Matthew 6:6–80	Year B—Thanksgiving Day
Matthew 9:35–38	Year A—Proper 6
	(2nd Sun. after Pentecost)
Matthew 11:25–30	Year A—Proper 9
	(5th Sun. after Pentecost)
Matthew 18:15–22	Year A—Proper 18
	(14th Sun. after Pentecost)
Matthew 20:20–28	St. James (July 25)
Mark 10:17–27	Year B—Proper 23
Luke 7:1–10	Year C—Proper 4
Luke 16:1–13	Year C—Proper 20
Luke 19:1–10	Year C—Proper 26
John 15:1–11	St. Matthias the Apostle
	(February 24)
	Year B—Easter 5
	Year B—Easter 6
John 15:12–16	Year B—Easter 6
John 16:12–15	Year C—Trinity Sunday
Acts 3:12b–21	Year B—Easter 3
Acts 11:1–18	Year C—Easter 5
1 Corinthians 1:10–18	Year A—Easter 3
1 Corinthians 2:1–10	Year A—Easter 5
1 Corinthians 3:1–11	Year A—Easter 6
1 Corinthians 12:1–11	Year A—Proper 1
	Year C—Epiphany
Philippians 4:4–9	Year C—Advent 3
	Year C—Thanksgiving Day
Colossians 3:8–17	Does not appear
2 Timothy 1:1–9a	Year C—Proper 22
James 2:1–13	Year B—Proper 18

TOPICAL INDEX TO SCRIPTURE PASSAGES